GRANDMA ESSIE'S COVERED WAGON

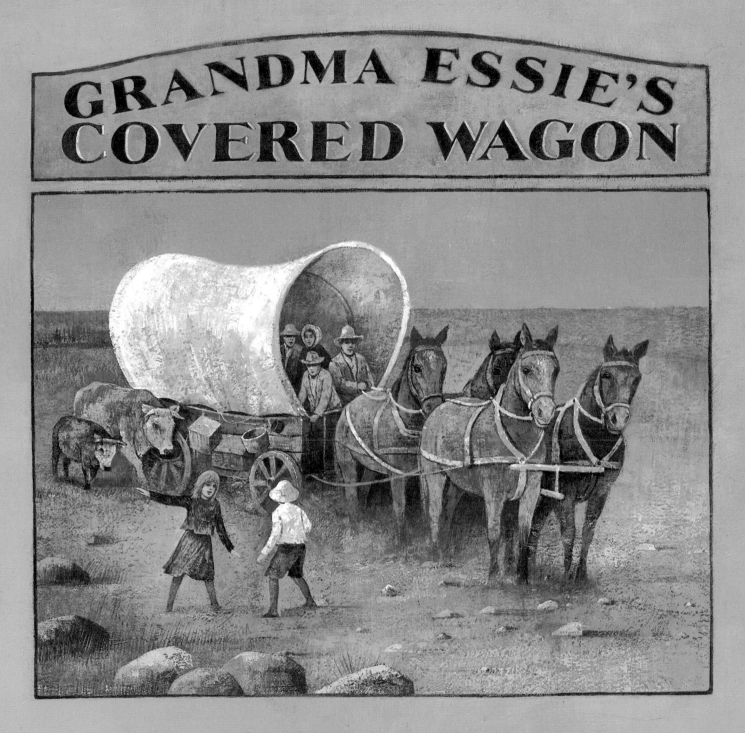

by DAVID WILLIAMS

illustrated by WIKTOR SADOWSKI

ALFRED A. KNOPF 🐕 NEW YORK

To the children, the grandchildren, and the great-grandchildren.
—David Williams and Essie Williams

THIS IS A BORZOI BOOK
PUBLISHED BY ALFRED A. KNOPF, INC.

Text copyright © 1993 by David Williams
Illustrations copyright © 1993 by Wiktor Sadowski
All rights reserved under International and Pan-American Copyright
Conventions. Published in the United States by Alfred A. Knopf, Inc.,
New York, and simultaneously in Canada by Random House of
Canada Limited, Toronto. Distributed by Random House, Inc., New York.
Manufactured in the United States of America
Book design by Elizabeth Nelson

2 4 6 8 10 9 7 5 3 1

Library of Congress Cataloging-in-Publication Data
Williams, David. Grandma Essie's covered wagon /
by David Williams ; illustrated by Wiktor Sadowski.   p.   cm.
Summary: Grandma Essie describes how her family left Missouri by
covered wagon looking for a better life and lived in Kansas and
Oklahoma before returning to Missouri.
ISBN 0-679-80253-3 (trade)   ISBN 0-679-90253-8 (lib. bdg.)
[1. Frontier and pioneer life—Fiction. 2. Middle West—Fiction.]
I. Sadowski, Wiktor, ill.   II. Title.
PZ7.W655925Gr 1993 [E]—dc20 90-24520

AUTHOR'S NOTE

As far back as I can remember, I've been listening to Grandma Essie's stories. Every summer my parents would take us kids "back home" to Missouri to sit on her porch swing and hear about things far different from what we knew. Grandma's father had once boarded Frank and Jesse James. She knew Wyatt Earp's cousin. And then there was the wonderful story of the covered wagon.

The stories Grandma Essie told from her childhood had a huge effect on me as a young boy, and in the fall of 1988 when Grandma came to visit, at the age of eighty-seven, I talked to her about capturing one in a book. Grandma was excited by the idea. All the details of her early days traveling in the covered wagon flooded back, and over the course of a week we went over them, meticulously re-creating each of the scenes. Here, then, is her story, in mostly her words, that I've helped shape and arrange.

The above photograph is of the family's Kansas farm. Twelve-year-old Essie is standing barefoot at the far right. To her left are sister Opal and her baby; sister Violet; brothers Kenneth and Jack; sister Stella; an unknown hired hand; Grandma Essie's mama; and finally Papa. Grandma remembers when the picture was taken—everyone was working in the fields when a traveling photographer happened by.

Grandma Essie has lived from the covered wagon days to the days when people fly to the moon. When you listen to her, I hope you can see the stern Midwestern landscape, feel the rowdy Kansas wind, and hear Grandma Essie's own voice as I hear it, wiser and stronger for having lived this life, but with an echo of the young girl who has never completely gone away.

I was born in a log cabin near Duenweg, Missouri, almost ninety years ago. There were six kids in our family—Stella, Opal, Kenneth, me, Jack, and Violet—and we lived in two little rooms. Papa worked as a hired hand, which didn't pay enough for us to buy nice things. But we didn't know any different and were happy—we had no idea Papa dreamed of something more.

Papa saved his money, then decided to go west and farm wheat. "There's lots of rich land in Kansas," he said, and soon we were all dreaming. Papa bought a frame wagon that farmers had used to haul crops. He bent wooden stays from one side to the other, nailed them down to form hoops, and stretched a white canvas over. As he worked, we watched our covered wagon rise, a magic ship that could take us anywhere.

Inside, Papa built shelves and Mama put in a little monkey stove. We loaded the wagon with all our clothes and blankets, and Kenneth hooked four mules to the front. Our calf, Molly, who was so gentle we kids used her for a pony, was tied to the back along with the milk cow. At last we were off to see the world.

Mama had made quilts, rugs, and comforts for everyone to sit on, and she rode with Violet on her lap. Opal, who was pregnant and got sick some of the time, sat between her husband, Arthur, and Stella. Kenneth rode up front with Papa. Jack and I rode wherever we felt like. Sometimes when we were restless, we'd even jump out and trot behind the wagon. We'd throw dirt clods at each other or ride Molly. There were lots of wild things outside—wolves, coyotes, foxes— but if they scared us, we'd just jump back inside and be safe.

We traveled through Kansas on dust and rock roads that went on forever. Sometimes we'd pass little farms and Mama'd buy eggs. She'd make pancakes in the morning out of scratch and brew Papa's coffee in a blue granite percolator. In the evenings we'd eat lots and lots of potatoes.

There were nights we never made it to a town and had to sleep on the earth. Mama would pull out every quilt, and we'd light a campfire. Stella would play the mandolin and sing songs like "From Jerusalem to Jericho" and "When the Roll Is Called Up Yonder, I'll Be There." We'd all join her on the chorus, then fall asleep together under the stars.

We went clear to western Kansas like that, to a little farm with an orchard and a red two-story house. Jack and I loved standing in the stairwell and yelling our names. We'd try to see who could be the loudest, our voices echoing back. Then we'd run every which way, our new home so big we thought it was a castle! We had beds to sleep on, and real cotton sheets. Mama sewed curtains out of old dresses. We scrubbed the walls and woodwork with rags, and soon the place looked good.

Most the land was prairie. It rolled on forever, like the back of some huge animal that might get up and run. The wind would whip out of nowhere, and sometimes Jack and I would grab the thick cushions off the sofa, take them outside, and hold them against our bellies. When the wind blew, we'd let go. The cushions would hold to us like magic!

It was hard for Papa to get the new place going. But wealthy wheat farmers *did* live in Kansas, and one little rich boy liked me. He invited me to his house for dinner one time, where there were all these cantaloupes and watermelons, but I was too bashful to taste any of them.

We had a horse named Major, who wouldn't get started once he'd stopped. One game was to pretend we were in the Big Top, then walk under Major or sit on his back. All the time, he'd just stand there, covered with the wild prairie flowers we'd decorated him with, nothing able to make him budge.

One day I was upstairs looking out our window, and there was the funniest sight I'd ever seen—a big black cloud winding up. I ran downstairs to Papa, who'd just come in from the fields.

"Take a look at this, Papa!" I cried. "There's something in the sky!"

At first he thought I was seeing things, but then he hollered, "It's a tornado!" and rushed us all to the cellar. The air was thick as a stampede. We huddled in the dark together, underground, our hands over our ears. Violet wouldn't stop crying.

A big river ran between our house and town. The tornado followed it, so we were saved.

We went barefoot through summer and fall and had to walk to school that way. Stella had always wanted a pair of white dress shoes, but Papa said no, we couldn't afford them. We sat with the other barefoot kids in the back of our one-room schoolhouse, the rich kids and their shoes up front.

Somehow, a front-row girl and I became friends. She had red hair and could really jump rope. She wore beautiful shiny black shoes, but I got to where I barely noticed them. We'd sing "Every Time I Go to Town Boys Start Kicking My Dog Around" and run through the playground, laughing.

Christmas Eve Papa went out and chopped down a small tree with bare branches. Mama had cut pictures out of the Sears-and-Roebuck catalog, and we hung them all over till the tree looked alive. She'd made rag dolls with button eyes and long yarn braids for us girls, and Papa had carved Kenneth a toy horse and made Jack a wagon. After all our popcorn was popped and eaten, all our cranberries strung, we sang "Away in a Manger" with Stella.

Then Christmas day, Opal had her baby! We tiptoed upstairs to peek at our first nephew, as big as a hand, healthy and screaming. Arthur was so happy about being a father he asked Stella to play her mandolin in the kitchen, then he danced.

Papa raised wheat, hay, and corn, but the second year in Kansas came a drought. Fields turned to dust. Plants wouldn't grow. Our horses went hungry, and the river ran dry. Jack and I could walk across it from mud bank to mud bank, seeing the dead fish and rounded river rocks. We'd pick those rocks up and hurl them just as far as we could, asking ourselves what happened.

Papa lost all his money, and we had to sell the farm. I said good-bye to my ducks. Our hound dogs, Papa gave to some neighbors. We auctioned off our horses, cows, and furniture, keeping only what would fit into the wagon, then we loaded it up and were gone.

Stella played "Diamonds in the Rough" as we bumped down the dusty road. There was just the sound of her fingers plucking strings and the sight of our own farm floating away.

We headed south, down to Oklahoma. Mama's folks lived near Oologah in a log cabin that reminded us of our home in Missouri. They were part Indian, Grandpa with his coal-black hair and mustache. He wore a felt hat with a big brim and played the fiddle, always wanting us kids to stay put and be his audience.

"You sit there," he'd say, "I want you to listen to this fiddle." But all *we* wanted was to go to the creek and swim.

Grandma'd tell us animal stories every night, smoking a clay pipe that we loved to light. Grandpa'd give us a big stick to put in the coals, then we'd get the tip of it on fire and touch it to the tobacco while Grandma puffed.

There was a big garden behind their cabin, and a kitchen that wasn't fastened on, and always plenty to eat. We camped at their place all summer and never wanted to leave.

But Papa heard about the oil fields in Big Heart, Oklahoma, and once more we loaded up the wagon. I tried to give Grandma the doll Mama'd made me. "I want Mary to have a real home like yours," I said, but Grandma thought Mary might need me, that I should take her.

Grandma and Grandpa waved to us from their porch as we left. Grandpa held his fiddle in one hand and Grandma cried.

Big Heart was a boom town. I'd never seen so many people or heard so much noise. The land was flat as a pancake, but the oil derricks that rose up every fifty feet made it look like a metal forest. Buildings were being put up left and right—banks, restaurants, saloons—and the streets were mud. There weren't any houses to live in. Papa set a tent up in a shantytown where other oil workers' families lived, and we parked the covered wagon. We sold our mules. Papa, Kenneth, and Arthur got jobs in the oil fields and were gone sunup to sundown, and always came home exhausted.

Stella began working for the Salvation Army to help raise money for the orphanage. As she played her mandolin and sang, oilmen would drop big silver dollars onto the drum. She sang in the streets all winter, then fell in love with the Salvation Army captain and planned to get married. But one day she took sick: just started coughing and couldn't stop. The doctor said she'd gotten ill from "exposure," being outside too long in the cold.

We prayed for her. We told her stories. We held her hand. Nothing would make her better.

One cold day in March, Stella died. Papa walked downtown and bought her a pair of white dress shoes, like she'd always wanted, to be buried in. But he wouldn't go to the funeral. He sat in the tent by himself while Mama and the rest of us went out past the oil derricks to the cemetery. The preacher said a few words, then we sang. And for a moment we all swore we heard Stella singing with us.

Mama thought I could get a job waiting tables, to help the family out. I was scared to try, but one day I walked into the Black Gold Restaurant and asked if they needed any help.

"How old are you?" this big woman asked.

"Fourteen," I lied.

"Well, let's see if you can work," she said, and soon I was carrying trays of food with my hands shaking the whole time and bringing home tips.

After a year in Big Heart we had saved enough to go. We bought two new mules and loaded the covered wagon for the last time. "We're heading back to Missouri," Papa said, and we moved to Seneca, on the Missouri-Oklahoma border. Opal and Arthur rented a house, and Papa bought a farm. It wasn't as nice as our place in Kansas, but we were so glad to have a home. Where the floors had cracks, Mama laid out rugs she'd made. She even wallpapered with newspapers to cover the spaces between the walls' wooden slats. And we went to bed nights feeling good.

There was a huge strawberry patch out back, so we went into business. When the berries ripened, we picked and boxed them, twenty-four to a crate, to be shipped out on the train. I made friends with a neighbor girl who worked for us, and sometimes before we started to fill a new quart we'd each write our name and address on the bottom. That way whoever bought the strawberries would know who we were.

One day Mama called me into the house. "A letter's come to you from New York City," she said. It was from a boy who'd gotten one of the strawberry quarts with my name inside. He said he wanted to marry me, but Mama wouldn't let me go.

Papa broke up the old covered wagon and sawed it to pieces. He made things from the wood—a table and chairs, a bookcase, a porch swing like the one we're sitting on.

I stayed in Seneca until I grew up and met your grandpa, an iron ore miner from Diamond. He was handsome. One day we went to Joplin and got married. Then we bought this house almost seventy years ago—here where I had my babies. My babies grew up, left home, and had their babies. But I never moved away.